DAVID HARSENT

Salt

FABER & FABER

First published in 2017
by Faber & Faber Ltd
Bloomsbury House
74–77 Great Russell Street
London WC1B 3DA
This paperback edition first published in 2019

Typeset by Hamish Ironside
Printed in the UK by TJ International Ltd, Padstow, Cornwall

A CIP record for this book is available from the British Library

ISBN 978–0–571–33786–6

FSC
www.fsc.org
MIX
Paper from
responsible sources
FSC® C013056

2 4 6 8 10 9 7 5 3 1

To Paul O'Prey

Contents

Author's note

The poems in this book belong to each other in mood, in tone, and by way of certain images and words that form a ricochet of echoes – not least the word 'salt'. They are a series, not a sequence. Although my intention was (and is) that the poems be read as wholly independent of each other, it became apparent, as I wrote, that some loose, disjointed narratives were developing: small broken chains of hint and harmony. I didn't resist that, though it was not part of any compositional plan.

D.H.

In the silence lies the secret.
ANTONIO PAPPANO
(from a talk on the Tristan chord)

I once went to the Metropolitan with Mark Rothko, and we'd look at a Rembrandt painting and the way Rembrandt bleeds to the edges. Take a look at a Rothko, the way he bleeds to the edges.
MORTON FELDMAN, *Essays*

SALT

She turned towards him, then she turned her back.

Early sunlight washed into the room. Then something like

the half-heard whine of flywheels, or

music composed for the gesture not the sunlight.

The sky brighter than before; rushes and salt-flats; white, broad-winged birds that landed standing, like angels, who are known by all to be salt-eaters.

The way you cut and draw a chicken, that tumble of guts
slipping into your hand; the way you try to make
the best of it; the way 'carcass' sounds when said out loud.

There was a hill in that place that no one ever climbed: accumulations of trash on the lower slopes, animal tracks after rain, songbirds in the scrub. Someone offered to rig an aerial walkway: 'As long as you don't set foot . . .' It was some lock-off in the contours, the way weather sat on the crest.

Raw rice and a line of salt, a jigger of salt at the threshold:
everything right, what with the hagstone and flax,
the fire banked so a flame could be caught and carried
to the unholy set-up locked off in the small back room.

Then the scapegoat 'in the full flower of his pathos'.
The friendless die first: little tumours seek them out
or their blood sickens in them. Their sure curative
is melancholy, but they sing and sing to hold off the dark.

He untangled the thing that had snagged in her hair, his hand
through a spectrum, spectral, blurring, a rail of fingers,
to lift the thing in her hair. It would rain that day, cloud low
to the hills, morning as nightfall, her window open to that.

As a closed fist is the lock of heaven. As a single word
can unpick everything. As pain has its own palette.
As water might be sweet or salt. The flatlands hold
a long horizon and the heat-haze flares in silence.

Simple tokens of death, grave-dolls, memento mori,

all so readily to hand: a stone marked like a skull.

Then she was in love and nothing changed although
she had less time for window-shopping
or drying her hair. They went to the theatre: he watched
as she watched the actors gesturing and talking to one another.

If only it were true that she'd had her first sight of him
as he crossed to the Café Bräunerhof, that they lied to one another
by agreement, that the house had mirrors in every room,
that they ate her afterbirth, that his hair turned white overnight.

When he entered her, and then his memory of that,

how slick it was and certain. She was empty of him, she said,

after so many years. His smile returned her smile.

The aged primigravida does the splits. Forceps are brought.
Her world of pain is such that she stands aside
to watch as the child is born to a season of rain and wind.
Selfhood is everything. Like mother, like son.

Love as subterfuge, or catalyst, or shibboleth, or lost light, or new light, or evidence of hidden music. 'Find Thalia and Melpomene held cheek to cheek, and there your mirror-self looks back at you and mine at me.'

In that silence he set out water and bread and salt.

He burned myrtle and hyssop. He wept. He called the quarters.

A photograph not of her, but someone like her.

A letter she never wrote: that bold facsimile.

The way they came into the room, this woman, then this,

and made themselves known to him. The way

silk brushes silk and lamps configure shadows.

In that tiny diorama, she waits at the open door.

She is perfect: nails and lips and hair. The windows

carry reflections of hills, and a river that seems to flow.

She has never been to such a place.

How can there live such loneliness in her?

That touch of madness in the blind-from-birth . . . Imagine
a bird in flight or physical beauty, both offered to corruption.

You can wake from a dream to a dream,

auditorium to roadscape, crush bar to crash site.

Voices go with you, in song or in sorrow or both.

A mark on flesh that could be anything. Something spoken or bitten back. A memory half-held that won't come good.

Helix pomatia inside a circle of salt: we endow

that purification, just as we scatter salt

over slugs to have them writhe in cleanliness,

just as we lavish salt on a flogged man's back.

The way lost things accumulate, the way they keep
a strict chronology . . . Unpossessed, they'll come
to a thickening of dust in stopless silence.

Her portrait hung out like a whore's shingle.

A bruised negative. Silhouettes walking the tideline.

Wind-blurred fugitives taken against the sun.

Remember this? Remember this? Remember

that cold delirium, the near-death feel of it?

A sidestep in the street, a soft-shoe shuffle, a hand
comes out to fend you off and then it's over.
Now rain is pocking the pavement where you walked
in that lost moment, slow city-rain breaking as splash and smut.

A salted seam, just fool's gold, leavings of a dream wherein
you give a true report of who you were, of what you could become.
In rainfall you're invisible, in sunlight the same, that's all
the dream gives up: a sense of place and sudden banishment.

He could feel his bare bones then, as if hung out

to a salt wind, his puppet-shadow loose-strung

and random music off him

so people might half-hear it as they passed.

A thickness in every breath.

The streets are white under hard sunlight.

'Where my shadow falls just short of me . . .'

Something inside him deployed. *Deployed* . . .
A full moon sat on the roof-tile, the sole focus
of his letter; her letter back was all chaff and fancy.
The throb in his fingertips was something and nothing.
It was too much to weep; too much and not enough.

Saltwater pearls, the diver's held breath,

five minutes, six minutes, his pulse a slow asdic.

They draw the damp between her breasts.

She thought that loss might be measured best in poundage,
stones dropped down on the board, stones and iron,
someone leaning in with a mirror to take the mist
of her breath, and her last words, 'More weight', as if
they might come face to face, and that the end.

'Seabirds': he spoke out loud to start the memory up.

Then 'Something in the sky', by which he meant

rain coming in from the unnaturally bright

seam of the horizon. Next he would have said 'Someone nearby'

had that person not been cloaked from him for years.

'A hand in front of your face,' they'd say, or else, 'There's none so blind.'

The place was picturesque, they all agreed on that.

A cat walked through unseen. You could stand with one foot

in —— the other in —— but report nothing, no, write nothing down.

Mirrors set at angles: he shrank in multiples.

His voice would only carry from one image to the next.

Folded in on himself. Her breath damp on the glass.

Deathbed, bed of dreams, sleep as departure,

the journey already mapped. The spectre of yourself

comes into the room: its careful tread, its gentle laughter.

She asked for a love-knot to be carved on the lid,

as if that had been their token, as if they'd talked it through.

To show him something of how it would look

she drew neatly on the fever-chart: a quick unbroken line.

As a butchered thing might be salted to preserve it.
As flesh might hold its own under that weight.
As skin might stiffen, as the raw might darken.
'Salt horse' or sometimes 'junk'. Headless and split,
nothing of tongue or teeth, nothing of salt-white eyes.

Into that other place, a bright machine, ratchets

clicking, the engine tiny for all that mass

of metal, crank-and-shunt, letting go a rich blue-black

skirl of smoke, its tracks a long meandros through the orchard,

apples falling, the reek of it bringing a shiver to the leaves.

He calculated sadness, types of sadness, sadness by degree,
the way a touch withdrawn might settle somewhere else.

The door was open and the room was dark.
There is a stillness that lies beyond sound,
beyond sense. It gathers to find its true weight.
Nothing survives it and it cannot break.

The garden was awash with green. It had seemed so before
but never on such a day as this. He was stricken by it.
Everything swarmed back to a vanishing point, beyond which
everything opened out to a garden awash with green
and sudden, anxious voices, all of them new to this.

'Without salt flesh gathers worms; and though flesh be our foe
we are commanded to sustain it. And we must afflict it.
Habete, inquit, sal in vobis. Offer me salt in every sacrifice.'

They found they could let slip their other selves, pale mavericks who would take to the streets dazzled by liberty, would talk to anyone, cross at blind corners, bed down in daylight.

'You can only come here once,' they said; 'the place is right
without you, by which is meant you'll never hold your ground.
Of course, it's known to you; of course you can smell the whin
and the view from the crest is almost what it was;
but those fault lines in the dell which you liked to think
were graves are really sinkholes as the women knew
who stood ready to keep you, scold you, catch you when you fell.
There are buzzards under the cloud-field. Hear them weep.'

First, that grand percussion as the pick-up
swerved and hit; then the creature down, legs going
at a flat-out run, its tripes starting to spill.
Sunlight on blood and diesel, trees turning in the wind,
the road empty save for this. Finally, he slept.

Salt to the stylite, salt to the anchorite. Burial
by hawk and crow, burial by iron and stone;
burial in kind – the fester of sin; then salt to the penitent.

He walked faster. He doubled his pace. He could hear
the sound of his footfalls, doors closing, voices
raised in chorus several streets away. A dog
was going at a swagger, head down, on the opposite side.
He had never wanted to be there: never wanted to come back.

A through-draught in an empty house, a curtain lifting
by a broken window, ash stirring in the grate, letters
on a table rising and settling. He lived with the image for days.
The letters were undated and the pen-work strong.

He cleared snow from the path and threw down salt.
He was conscious of oxygen, then: the word, also the way
his breath came back at him to leave a trace
of ice on his upper lip. This soon after dawn,
the sleepers in the house fixed like the dead, except one
who turned in her dream looking for elbow-room, her voice
just short of reaching him, the snowfall soundless, the salt
finding its way, the scuff of his boots in all that ghostliness.

That morning, he saw things differently, as if
last light still quartered the house and she herself
at the pivot, seeming to wait for what would happen next.
They were motionless, yes, but it was more than that.
He knew she would gather in whatever he left unsaid.

What held him held him fast. It was rainfall
against the glass that brought him back.

Laid out in drills: monkshood, blood lily, black
henbane, skullcap, the pasqueflower.
And these the least of it: 'My poison-garden'.

Bread, water, salt: the sin-eater's little kit, so easily
unpacked, unpacked and spread, spread
pubis to clavicle, and a fire in the hearth kept in,
and silver handed over and all there standing to watch
whose tongues tipped their teeth as he dipped and took the salt.

They eavesdropped on one another. He read her mind. She wrote him notes that could have come from anyone.

His mirror image blanked him; he turned instead
to the image in the window, weather as aide-memoire:
'One drop of wine, wherewith wild rain has mixed'. A little death
came in at the mirror's edge: bed, bed-bottle, bed-
side lamp, the yellow-orange light seeming a stain.
Mourners arrived to sample the last of his air.

That sudden stillness will catch you out,
like driving into a cul-de-sac, becoming lost
among trees, not knowing the language, going naked
in a house you used to know, or think you did.

The hallway was empty, was endless. There were doors on either side. You can imagine it, can't you? The bare boards, the dado rail, a glint off the brass doorknobs, the way it fell away to fog and blur, the scent of almonds.

Salt burns blue-green. Feathers burn rank. Just as milk

has a blue undertone in certain lights, just as

a whiff of mildew will give you back that book,

that house, the way the path broke to woodland, night

holding back, some hint of what came next.

The grime was expected, was just as before, a film
to the glass that seemed albumen-and-dust,
the world outside cast in sepia under streetlights.
Where else to be? Where else to come to? Everything
to hand, everything as it should be, as hoped-for, even
the familiar low drone that nightly runs in the wainscot,
something like plainsong or the music of small machines.

Rags of piety, the way your mind ransacks the celestial

and how a bird in flight locks off in memory . . .

Coldness was a blessing to you then: hoar frost underfoot,

ice over slow water, the way things dimmed in white.

Weep for it now, yes weep, it can't come back.

Slight movements betray him – that turn-and-turn-away,

the caught reflection in the kitchen window,

a tremor that finds its way to the water in his glass.

It broke from a stand of corn, bald-eyed, smelling the scorch.
There are other ways to describe this; they might involve
that running swerve as the fire nudged it, the way its flank
singed: fur rumpling to black, how it then held up,
hectic but still, as smoke flowed over the sun.

Bone-scrape, as if a saw-like thing or claw-
like thing, deckle-edged, had been laid to the thick
of the joint and drawn hard back, drawn down and back.
That curlicue to Mother Dark, the knuckle-bone to the drum.

Horehound and lupin, stewed; salt, of necessity;

lees and leavings, slops, bone-ash, dieback and dreck;

hemp; her blood; the ejaculate of the damned.

A bird tethered to a wheel, wryneck, the bird of madness.

Now crank the wheel, you can draw down love with this.

Ab ovo: screams, release, himself into the world,
knowledge of him, the naming, moorland weather
starting a sweep of snow across the glass, and on the sill
flowers that should be roses but never will be, never were.

A sudden dizziness as if blood-loss, a face come back

to memory after years of banishment,

from the parapet a view of the turning world.

A certain book open at a certain page: perhaps
had fallen open. He knew there was nothing in that:
spillikins, the turn of a card, the spin of a knife.

Old photographs laid out like this, her hand

going in among them, faces coming back at her,

a fragment of speech – something less

than half-said that carried its meaning entire.

A radio from two streets away: music for the dying;

bruise-dapple on one arm, the other sleeved in blue.

What else can't you see? How the bed

has been turned from the light? How flesh is ripe

to fall from the bone? How fear is mute?

A secret life in which only the names are the same,
where the right house is found in the wrong street, where cafes
are full of people who look unlike themselves, where voices
blur and break. In a pixelated world they go by touch.

They salted the streets and posted red weather-alerts.
He turned her out of bed and there it was, the little fiction
he'd planned for – her reflection held four-square
in the bedroom window, driven snow under the coming dawn.

The stark repetitions of prayer that always seemed somehow spur of the moment. Once on his knees he lurched into sleep as if in a dream of falling.

A story for children, she said, everything laid out:
'Once in a country far from here . . .' so simple, so easy to say.
Years before she had gambled her life on that,
not the story so much as the way it might be told.

Then it sank in him, a tremor that went so deep

as to play on his backbone, to ring on his spinal cord.

No pucker on his skin, no eyelid-tic,

but something like a blush

on his fingertips as he laid them to the keys.

The phone call went for nothing, things were set
as if the weather had a hand in it, day-long
rainfall, uncommon greyness drawn across her face.

The taste of sin to the gourmet: a nip of salt,

as it might have come off the cutting-edge of a knife,

tip of the tongue going out,

blood-and-salt, one version of betrayal.

Ice-crystals across his eyes, a broken flow, the world
beyond the window sliding in slow dissolve.
What lies below bulks up but can't break through.

That far country we all have at heart, where Life-in-Death
will bring our drinks to poolside tables, where
beds will seem to fall away beneath us,
where love will come to nothing and again.

'The curtain dropt and Bel-imperia dead'. Snowfall
thinning to sleet becoming ice; he drove
feathering the wheel, soft on the brake,
as they talked it through, her clever step downstage,
the knife delayed, the way she found the light . . .

Her sudden, silent prayer was commonplace –
to betray but do no harm, to admix guilt with love
and that way get the best of it, to let each salty lie
roll on her tongue, to gamble with heartbreak, to give
an account of herself that would seem most like herself.

Frame it up like this: a door, an inner door, a room
held ready, bare walls, weight
of silence, a glass of water cut by sunlight.

They found somewhere to eat. He went at it head down two-handed, suddenly ravenous and lost to her then: a moment she'd expected, had waited for, had wanted.

A word spoken in darkness; she woke

to everything as it was, her dream-self dressed to kill,

right place, right time, the way she turned his head.

Low skies bringing rain in off the sea, the deep odour
of wet tarmac. How often have you been here before?
Those two on the boardwalk going in step, an old man
waiting to cross, the girl muffled in blue,
hand raised to flag a taxi . . . actors edging the real.

Her spittle was wine and salt. Later, he took salt
from the tip of her breast with the tip of his tongue.
They could eat whenever they chose, they could go
from place to place without having to say why, or sit
in total darkness close enough to touch but never touching.
They thought they might cut each other's hair to get
the sudden lightness in that, the flow, the naked neck.

More than it seemed, but less than she'd hoped for: a voice calling her back. The journey from street-door to street left her breathless. Where she goes, the pollarded trees raise their stumps, a thin hosanna turning in the wind.

Sloe-light sometimes, or the drone of flies as they crowd
a slather of shite, or the sea with its nag-nag-nag.
No one comes, in that final hour, to warn or console.
Things move as is the way of things: weird slow-motion dance.

A blind house: no door to the world outside,
every window sealed, a web of hallways, rooms
littered with absences. Heartless geometry.
People stand in the street and call your name.

Drinkers at corner tables, the bar in day-long twilight, unspoken monologues. Tomorrow, this will have changed and there's no way to second-guess that shift, or know how well the other version is likely to hold up.

She puts down her book and lifts her drink, a cloud
of dew on the glass, a circle of salt on the rim;
she takes the scent of tequila first, then drinks. It might
be years before she goes back to the book, those lines
and layers, deaths and denials, that tallyman hero.

Music at every turn, music by accident, a voice between the phrases, between the notes, calling, calling, and this not song but touchstone, blind bargain, last chance.

There's a shadow in from under the door. Can you see it yet:
shadow of slow-onset, contagion's mission-creep?
Voices held to a monotone, the painting, the clock,
hanging clothes, aerials and ridge-tiles, cirrus, cirrus.

A roadside saltstack sculpted by rain; go past at a crawl and – yes –
that warp is her likeness, fixed there and webbed with darkness
by surface spray. Come back to it, park up, take your time.

The want of emptiness as if it were a place, a house, a room

within the house, as if to stand unmoving at the dead

centre of the room would usher in

yourself as abstract, all potential gone, all remedy,

light falling into light, that subtle wind the winnow of your soul.

A face peering in, a naked form set flat on a bed or bench, a hand
turning a key. The dream's ironwork and dross, its shaft
and dead drop. You come back changed, singing the life you left.

Now the flat of her knife between skin and flesh. She's up
on her toes as if she were dancing and dips
the salt-box for savour. How could he match the moment:
his ill-chosen gift, his one word out of turn?

Repetitions of water over stone unseen,

the dog turning on its owner, street-dust,

some shelving in the heart, a loss of light, just this.

In one version he died in pain,

in another she held him as he 'slipped away'.

Something like a wolf, something like

a figure in cap and bells, laughter from the room

beyond that room (wild laughter), something like

the song she might sing. The night sky ran in clusters.

As a tarantula moves, she said, or else a rat

when you come at it with a broom. The stooping shadow,

the countdown, the scuttle-and-lock, the love-cry.

A place where the sun never quite comes up, where birds are voiceless, where all water is salt water. They go naked, the 'inhabitants'; their voices might be machine-made, a sweet soft hum that will draw you on even as you make to turn away.

The sureness of animals is something
of the true magic. Turn back to your plate;
you have what you need of flesh:
the muscle-flex, the swerve before the drop.

Nothing but want, nothing to give, and this lifelong:
out on a two-lane blacktop as night comes in,
as rain comes in, unchanging from then to now,
the nightbirds, the long lights, the world apart.

The hands of the puppeteer are chafed by love. His people dance and clap and jabber, and kiss by knocking heads. Their names are known only to him. If they lie to one another his fingers ache. Husband and wife and lover and stranger and fool: they fall into themselves, find common ground, go side by side.

Blood-toil, brooch out of bone given over from wolf or bear,
paper-thin and done by firelight: the scrape of flint, the dense,
deep odour of smoke. It could only have come to him
by theft. She pinned it on and the ground gave under her.

Flick-book flick-flick-flick-book: the on/off love-affair

the pratfall the naked man going over the wooden horse

the screaming nurse the bathing belle: she held it up before his very eyes.

Deathbed-reading ready-stacked spine-out,
Apophthegmata Matrum, Q's Songs, etcetera. There would be
Lindt 'with a touch of sea-salt' (and why not?)
drug imperious and drug of choice. *I observed the doctor sniffing*
like someone testing a bad egg: 'There's fever here.' Daylight
weighs on the air in this account; or else air weighs on the light.

Under an open sky: the beast brought out and tethered,
dumb submission to the butcher's hand. The gutters
slope to drains, the runaway goes to vats, the butcher's
hand hangs by his side, its own fell instrument. What is it you lack
that you should think like this? Sun out of cloud, laughter
from beyond the compound, the swipe of the butcher's hand.

And that was the way of it, intermittent silences,
a shutter clattering in the wind,
the unanswerable telephone. In her final letter
she had written *vitrea fracta*, wanting to explain
how certain things would soon become impossible.

Dust-devil, twister, cyclone, clean sweep,

she is locked-off in this and the place is dark just as

a pebble is dark at its centre . . . then her prophecy-in-song,

eyes wide open, his hand moving across her mouth.

Down a salt-track to the sea, red-eyed and shaking.
Happy birthday! Happy birthday! As birds hold up
against the wind, as light drains off in rainfall,
so you lag and diminish, blind to what's at your back.

Goddess or nurse at the bedside, a painting of this
done in misty blues and whites. The patient
has seen out the night. The patient's breath
is on the air but will not resolve in paint. The patient
is too pale and thin to be seen. If only she'd leave her chair
and go to the window. If only we could test the weather,
black scaffolding of trees, sunlight off the snow.

For the sleepwalker, music, or music of a sort,
carried on lines of darkness to bring him out,
bare feet on bare boards, soft hands of the psychopomp,
the certainty of descent as if it were a dream, as if
he could wake himself on the turn of the stair or at least
in the kitchen with its hooks and blocks, safe ground.

There was laughter about the place, small, subtle laughter, laughter
of the household gods, gods of lintel and hearth . . .
Headaches, hidden malice, an issue of blood. Put up
shutters against the sun; live long in that faux dusk.

Wind-driven salt in the crevice of a rock is how
memory works: image, invention, regret. It maddens
with its unknowable language, sudden reversals,
shoreline, skyline, cityscape, landscape . . . There are those who wake
with the whole thing fixed at the forefront of their minds:
a stage-set, people held in a frozen moment who will break
to action soon, one fearful, one laughing, one turning her back.

Blackwater tidewrack, as if the river could get this far
with its backwash litter of skin and bone, as if broadwinged birds
overflew it, their downdraft stirring whirlpools, as if light
came hard and slant across the floodplain, as if your window
opened onto this which is 3D micro-sleep, is dream as blitzkrieg,
short-circuits sparking your nerve-track, your head a beacon.

Slow sacrament of cheese and olive oil and bread, the creep
of sundown-sunlight on the wall. 'How safe do you feel
at times like this?' He bared his teeth. A thing flew in
at the transom, bird or bat. 'It's like looking at clear water
through clouded glass.' They were far off from anywhere.

To be sightless and speechless, to be the last of the lost, to be left with nothing underfoot, the day on all sides darkening (*Your head, your poor head* she would say), a blue flame in a glass jar, and then words given in hope, those small collisions, their afterlife in song.

Sanctum sanctorum, bad breath, smegma, spillage and swill.

Diary of the suicidal child. Broken glass, graffiti, blood.

Ungovernable anger of the convert. Dogshit, the bloom on rot,

the locked book broken and burned. A loop-tape, mirrors . . .

It was the inner dream, he knew that from the shop-fronts,
the peeling paint and scabbed clapboard. The outer dream
had brought him here through a wilderness of roads
and road-signs. He found his way, a man on a compass-point;
there were hard winter shadows, a telltale trace of salt
on the paving stones. The fault line between the dreams
was broken sleep or apnoea or sudden white-screen breakdowns . . .
So it returns, the bare brickwork, the cold-hearth-home-from-home.

Your *vade mecum* has it: witch hazel against the wounds
of childbirth, black cohosh to bring in her milk, asafoetida
against excessive bleeding, borage against melancholy . . .
How will she cope with this soak of healing, this solace?

She turns, her hand held out, and then it fades. She turns
and you see more of it: the garden bench, the cat,
the new growth in the bay tree; then it fades.
And when she turns you almost have it whole:
bright eyes, small sly smile, something said but fading.

If warm blood has a salt tang, and if sunlight fetched
a bright seam to the curtain's overlap, or a chainsaw
had been at work somewhere nearby, it might be said
that she lay flat out face up legs spread as if
dropped from a great height, and somehow unmarked.

A stain that runs under everything, that travels with you,

that puddles where you pause, marks what you touch,

that carries its own colour, its own scent hot and heavy

which is, you think, death in the offing, but no – no –

it's what shows up with death, comes hand in hand, comes

only to mourn, love in disguise, low note of heartache.

As a dog can tell a coming storm; as someone you love
might pass you in the street; as music is nothing more
than aide-memoire; as sorrow hangs in still air;
so it is that you know this house, this room, your childhood bed.

Thorn as a symbol of the risen Christ, thorn as ill luck
when brought indoors, thorn in the flesh
that she picked out with a needle, lifting a flap
of skin then bearing down on the place so it came
with a squeeze of blood, and thorn
on her mind when she knelt and turned her back
face-down in a pool of morning sunlight.

Salt-wife up to her thighs in the tideline-chop,

loosening her scalp where it binds at the fontanelle.

Better to shed this dream on waking

than spend your life in want of her.

If you laugh in your sleep, you'll be heard. If you back-
track you'll be second-guessed. You are held in the moment,
raw-boned and open to touch: bird in lime, rat on a glueboard.

He was wearing a dead man's coat: knee-length, snug,
the lining rich, shot-silk in midnight blue. 'As I thought,'
she said, 'a perfect fit. Of course, you look nothing like him,
nor do you have that rangy, loose-limbed stride
or straightness of back.' One side-pocket was sewn up,
in the other, a letter. He threw it away as he left.

Her blood blossomed in the water-trap and her voice
came as a rolling echo from an empty room in a place
long since lost to the world. His ghost tugged to be free.
He lay all day in bed, people he knew or once knew
filing past and fading as they reached the limit of his love.

He wept for no good reason, reason he felt was the least of it,
soon enough reason would pass him by. He was struck
by how leaf-fall continued after dark and woke at 4 a.m.
with a memory of pain but no bruise or else none visible.
Slow wind. Half-moon. Something from the broken-ended dream.

That he left a trace on her, salt-bright; that she gave
the taste of it back to him; that nothing was good enough:
rainwash on the wall, the hand-to-mouth of their day-to-day.
She stepped away and the space between them sagged.

What they did to him was unwatchable; what they did
lay far beyond belief – daytime terrors, waking dreamtime,
the lock-up, breeze-block walls, chain-drag, the Black & Decker
kicking in, winged creatures, they sing as they work.

The dead are given permission to walk among us.
They smile dead smiles, they have no need for speech.
The familiar goes for nothing. Each evening
they hold up to our windows their silent, smiling children.

Something shifted under his skin, it puckered as might a worm
going slither-and-tuck close to the nape of his neck, then up
past the cheekbone and on to the sill of his eye to gorge
on the image trapped there, the last of her, the last lost thing.

Graves under bramble and a wet light through the trees.
A quietness something like stealth or sudden absence; it seemed
to gather and disperse. Rat-run, ground for stray dogs, a place
where lovers come to be swallowed whole by half-light.
You could lie down here on thorn, on stone, and find your match.

Salt-slip in a field of salt. Men in white are raking it. They turn as one at the edge of the field as if going about from the lip of the world. They work bare-headed under the sun; white light hammers back from the tillage; wind-taken airborne dust, they breathe it, they smile white smiles, white teeth, white fingernails, white eyes, they are salt-stiffened, they go as one, they carry a song in their heads but salt thickens their tongues, they cannot sing, there is just this field of salt below a birdless sky, they rake, they come to the edge.

Music in every room and no one listening. Words that fall into silence.
Nothing abides, no, and nothing prospers. How will you stock
your newfound emptiness? A moment re-remembered endlessly,
a chain of echoes in which you accuse and are accused in turn.

Smell of the alley you might have to come to: piss and piss and piss.
Might have to live in, might have to make your home:
piss and piss and everything you own.
Dark trench above the brickline, funnel for rainfall,
cloud-sluice, night sky broken and running red.

Instant afterburn of gin, dim procession of memories,
ambition lost to circumstance, blame and blame again.
These are not nightbirds as you think, but thin-pitched
voices of the once and always abandoned come down
to hooks and tongues. They flock in the bankside trees,
harbouring cruelty. There will be nights given over to this.

Is it right that you should sit here at the window, as if a traveller,
the rain coming hard and slant against the roadside trees,
the sound of it all one steady note, and you cut off from speech,
or so it seems, your ghost draped over your bones? How far
have you come? What more do you need to know?

Saltwater remedy, your body soft to the bone,

but then emerge to daylight, glitter of silica,

a frame-by-frame fracture-and-gather as you come

to yourself piecemeal, full and fine and bright and pitiless.

Twice told, as if it were life-and-death to know
that we walk above the course of an underground stream
walking blind, a snag to our foot-soles coming up through the asphalt,
as if knowing might help second-guess that dream-track,
might bring us to a place apart, stranded in some junk yard
at nightfall, bricked in, the graffiti livid and bleak and personal.

Rough sleepers turn away and fold into their stench,
scholars of the omphalos and arsehole. Go by, go by.
Soon they will rise as one, a long silhouette
snaking between tail lights, and start the final journey
to Axis Mundi. The pavement artists have your likeness,
that coal-black broadcloth suit, that whisky-stagger.

In one room a man working, in another
a woman sitting still. Marriage bed, deathbed,
cold kitchen. Your guided tour of the house.
The staircase, the turn of the stair, a room kept dark.
Look in from outside: your shadow falls to the floor.

She was undermined by a memory of snow that soon became
a need for snow. Look at it from where she stands: a blank
field, the sky turned in on itself, the last drop already taken.
There are flights of birds, wind-driven, and she's a step
beyond where she meant to be, not stranded, not abandoned,
though she asks herself how and why and who will come to me?

There in a salt-mist, in fever-dreams, his image
caught between glass and silvering,
powerless, motionless, breathless, enraged . . .
The mirror trembles. His eyeballs smudge the skim.

It lay with him like a curse, a voice out of silence,
and he lifted up in the dark, propped on one elbow
as if he had suddenly come to life. He thought
he could taste blood on his lip, a subtle wet,
and felt what would have been the attendant pain,
or an echo of that as if he had suddenly come to life. As if
he had suddenly come to life, he rose and went to the door
in the dark; it opened onto a house where people might
have been sleeping, locked-off in dreams that shed a cool
blue light in a soundless place, and loveless, faultless . . .

Her fetch is heavy-eyed and pale, and blonde after a fashion.
She has you in mind. She has given you a name. She will vouchsafe
the tight little nub of her arsehole: it's nothing to her.
You will stand in need of her. She will learn to be whatever suits you best.

As pen to paper, so razor to strop; it's written in blood.

'Since music is in the offing,' he said, 'I would sooner wait on that.'
What would it be but avoidance of harm and a place in the coming dark
and the sky in flood and everything in the swim?

Salt-flats of dream of memory of dream . . . limitless horizons
and out on the utmost rim (can you see?) a house
as white-on-white abstract except for the room-within-a-room
which can't be seen but can be known, white being one thing
in sunlight another under moonlight, not oblivion, not revival,
and the soul's song across that windless landscape, unheard;
by night the heart-stopped silence, by day the rising glare.

Hanging rain on a slow wind, open your mouth, give up,
look back the way you came, give up, understand
there is nothing to be done, you will never want
for anything, you will be loved, it will come to you
as rain holds up on the wind, open your mouth, look back,
yes, you are spoken-for, yes, marked down for love, give up
your mouth to the rain, do nothing, you will never be in want.

She walked from street to street; she might as well have been cloaked
and masked; it seemed to her that she left her reflection in windows,
her breath as stain; the blood let go from her womb, a sudden jolt.
It's fine, she told herself, I'll arrive and be welcome as before.
My children will put me to bed. I'll sleep with the light on.

A jackhammer at work on the party wall, birdsong, engines, voices from the street: glorious constancy, as if the world outside could hold up, as if it could sustain, insist, draw down notions of itself, be word and music, be always touchable.

Here is your space, lie down or stand or sit, it will take your shape.
Be still if you can. Look into yourself for what is soft and spoiled,
for pulp, for that dark damage. There was a morning, once, sunlit
and you in the full of it, unimpeded, set up to be lost then lost,
falling in with those near-broken by love, falling in
with those given over to harm. Be still if you can: you will hear
the sound of yourself, blood purling along the bone; and it might
come to you that regret has an afterlife, that it stains and stays,
that what you have left is what you now hold to your heart
which is nothing and less than nothing in this fog of exile.

They weighed the human soul – twenty-one grams – a tremor
on the air becoming trance, becoming nimbus. No. It is a plummet,
drawing down to its harbour beside the heart. It is Breath
and Word, they said. No. It is pig-iron and salt. The dying
feel its slow lift as riddance, a bar of darkness hoisting against the light.

To live in silence, to write a white book, to go
touchless from place to place,
to shuffle off your skin, the mask of your face
under its hank of hair still placid and empty-eyed.

The wall unbricked, last line of the last graffito broken,

words from the foot of the cross if you want to read it that way,

or mendicant children tagging home ground; they lie up

over gratings, go among the early-evening crowds

with their chants and threats. See here, they have fouled their nests,

they won't come back. They stake out bridges, shopfronts, back alleys,

bed down in dirt. Bandits of the inner-city footings, they dig in.

'Will you live in memory? Will that be you at your best?
Will you wake with your other life intact, an open book
in one hand, the other lightly cupped between your legs
(pose of a houri), bed set so you find your face in the mirror?
Does this image come back to you as it does to me?'

This last: the house on a summer's evening, a winter's evening,
an evening in spring, his hand outstretched, the room
unlit (are you there, do you see what I mean?)
I think he is singing to himself, I think he is almost lost
to himself, I think he feels the slow turn of the world
how things about him quake and merge and liquefy.

Once and once only, a Brocken spectre, mere luck,

or else his mirror image stepping down and reaching out.

Rainfall in woodland, look hard at this,

stand in the drench to disappear, be voiceless,

be still, leave yourself there lost to sound and sense.

Finally, then, how last light fails as it settles on empty streets,
how dawn light fails, how it fails to bond, how dew
comes in as salt to scar the windowpane. Now walk
into the world outside with hand to heart; how slight
things seem, how close to that slow fade, the edge of sleep,
blur of lost focus, of memory beyond remembering.
You are loved of course, though it doesn't tell on you.

Trash alleys, dog-bark echo, last train out, the whole thing
air-drawn, but he keeps it intact, even the chill of sweat
that comes to the small of his back. The one word he speaks
to break the silence holds on the air long enough
to remind him of what he meant to say. The place is his to map
or tear down, from the 7-Eleven out to the no-limit blacktop.

Rat's foot on litter, on crusted slime, deeper
in reek and rot, a house you used to own become
nothing but passageways, hidden doors, stairways
that come to nothing, the air thick with spores and spoil;
it's sure you will turn at last to this scant evidence.

Oil and salt, pestle and mortar, a mash of herbs,
the shadow of a hand over this lost memory
(false memory) of women singing as they work,
pale rhomboid of light from a tall window
falling across the tiles, the sound of a whisk
in batter, the soft tap-tap of a pot lid on the stove,
everything set up and ready for breakage.
They sense that breach in the air but don't look up.

When a man in a tunnel must go on all fours, must go on,
air breathable but rank, eyes functioning but fixed
on the little bowl of darkness where light will fall and fail
when he makes his way, where nothing is kept from memory
nothing from sorrow, where echoes roll in that narrow: the dead
sound of the dead in full voice when he makes his way
and lost things come to hand, unused, immaculate.

Fear of hidden illness took him, and this was bred in the bone.

His night-walks mapped the city. Nowhere was far enough.

Nightscape of the sea, salt moon, cliff edge, how a man might take flight, spring-heeled and somehow airborne arms spread to the updraught, held high in the drop and a skyscraper vigil much the same, and the same from the top tier of a multi-storey car park, neon slick on a wet road, the trundle of waves, of traffic, freefall.

Signs of mortality: spider-veins, a naevus,

webbed on the inside thigh; a slowness in rough weather

so the heart seems to take on weight; dreams

where the dreamer intervenes to face down death.

There is no good advice for this. Go out early.

Wear a clean white shirt. Get there before she wakes.

As lewd nocturnal, as night-nurse, as someone to fetch

whisky and pen and paper and books on a dolly-dish

and photographs given in sequence so the tale is properly told

and Item 1 and Item 2 which must remain unnamed

and something to eat you won't eat and something to wear you won't wear.

As you open your mouth to speak, she lowers herself

onto you, moth-soft, and you take yourself up into her as a last resort.

He fingers the wind, a piano, it might be
a violin, a flute. Birds overhead, birdcall his music.
A satchel of scraps and snaps, he lets them go
to clutter the sky. He's rocky with analgesics.
To be out in bad weather is all that's left to him.

It might be a painting, *Debitum Naturae*, faces
gone blank with watching, blank with waiting, everyone
breathing in unison so it seems, hands lost to purpose, the wet
of their eyes giving back the light which is, let's say,
light from a part-open door. What now? What now? What now?
Between white sheet and white pillow, a hardening stare.

Waking at the dead hour, blinds open to moonlight,
your silhouette sharp-cut on a wall white as bone, as salt:
both this and a vision of this, one set down
on the other, the moon itself and a version of itself,
the room a place you might come to or soon abandon;
and it rises, now, a pain behind your eyes, touching
the sclera, touching the nerve, rag-ends of a dream
where you find your lover in her husband's bed.

See it out, see it out: each breath a deadweight
each passing thought masquerading as your last,
all night wide-eyed in that backwash of white/blue light
so your pulse goes with the tides (and her blood, too)
when the ache in a turning wave is a vacancy in air
as if music might break the silence, or silence be endless.

Acknowledgements

Some of the poems in this book have appeared in *Agenda*, *Compass*, *High Window*, *London Review of Books*, *Next Review*, *Ploughshares* (USA), *Poem*, *Poetry* (USA), *Poetry London*, *Smartish Pace* (USA).

The poem on page 41 modifies a line by Seamus Heaney. The poem on page 43 is lifted, and adapted, from the *Ancrene Riwle*. The poem on page 56 takes a line from a poem by Conrad Aiken. The poems on pages 87 and 172 make use of lines from my versions of Yannis Ritsos.